A Craft Studio BOOK

STAMPING & PRINTING

20 CREATIVE PROJECTS

ÉMILIE GREENBERG
& KARINE THIBOULT-DEMESSENCE

Photographs: Claire Curt
Stylist: Karine Thiboult-Demessence
with Émilie Greenberg

Thames & Hudson

INTRODUCTION

Stamping and printing are an easy and accessible way to be creative. They require few materials, and can produce surprising and original results, sometimes strikingly simple and sometimes deceptively sophisticated. This book will show you how to print attractive contemporary motifs on items such as pillowcases, aprons, placemats or trays, using everyday objects like a potato, an apple, a piece of string or a cork. You can print your own wrapping paper with beads, create a painting with foam stamps or upcycle an everyday object to give it a new lease of life. This is a great way to add a lively, modern touch to your home, without breaking the bank.

CONTENTS

TIPS & TECHNIQUES

Here is a list of the materials you will need to make the stamps and projects shown in this book.

You can make stamps from

Alphabet pasta shapes
Clay
Cord
Cork
Cotton buds
Date stamps
Foam paint pouncers with circular ends
Foam sheets
Fruits and vegetables
Fuse beads
Kitchen roll tube
Lace
Leaves
Linocut sheet
Pastry cutters
Patterned glassware
Pencil rubbers
Phillips screwdriver
Piping nozzles

Other tools you need

Acrylic stamping blocks
Cardboard
Chopping board
Contact glue
Cotton buds
Craft knife
Double-sided sticky tape
Felt-tip pens (in various colours)
Foam blocks (for applying paint)
Gouges (for linocutting)
Greaseproof paper
Kitchen paper
Paint mixing sticks

Paintbrushes
Paper plates
Peg boards for fuse beads
Pencils
Pure bleach
Ruler
Scissors
Spray glue
Sticky tape
Tailor's chalk
Toothpicks
Tracing paper
Water-based matt varnish

Inks and paints

Acrylic paint
Ceramic paint (water soluble)
Fabric paint
Gouache paint
Ink pad (for paper and fabric inks)
Spray paint

Preparation

Before beginning to print, make sure you protect your work
surface with an old tablecloth or piece of cloth.

Always work on a flat surface to ensure that the motifs are
firmly stamped onto your paper or fabric. Make sure that
your materials and tools are clean and in good condition.
Be especially careful to use new blades in your craft knife
and steer clear of poor-quality paintbrushes that lose their
bristles. When printing wrapping paper, put heavy objects on
its corners to keep it flat.

The keys to success

The secret to printing clearly defined motifs is to avoid
putting too much paint on the stamps - and, above all, don't
dilute the paint with water! Apply paint with a flat brush,
to prevent any accidental blots or lines. Before printing your
motif, try it out on a support similar to the one you are going
to use. If printing on wood, try testing it on a surface that
is usually hidden from view, like the back of a tray.

When using an ink pad, you must press the pad onto the stamp and not the other way round, or else the stamp will be overloaded with ink. Be aware that fluorescent pink and white are greasier than other colours, so use them sparingly and make sure they dry thoroughly.

As a general rule, you should press down firmly and evenly, but without squashing the stamp (and take special care when using polymer clay, because things can get messy). The rougher the printed surface, the fuzzier the resulting motif. You can experiment with the effects produced by different surfaces, and use them to make your designs more distinctive.

A solid base for your stamps

Some stamps have to be fixed onto a support. Use contact glue or double-sided sticky tape to stick them securely onto a solid base such as a board, a piece of wood or heavy cardboard, a child's building block, a coaster or the lid of a jar. You can also buy acrylic stamping blocks made specifically for this purpose from craft stores.

Types of stamp

When you're making your own stamps, different materials suit different surfaces. Rubber, for example, won't work on either wood or metal, while clay can only be used on textiles. In contrast, foam stamps can be used on all types of surfaces (paper, wood, fabric and more). Some of the projects include a note stating if a particular design can be used on an alternative material.

Stamping with objects

Sometimes a design can be created by printing with an object. For example, a motif can be created by pressing a decorative piping nozzle directly into polymer clay, or a lacy pattern can be printed on a tin by covering the surface with lace and applying a layer of spray paint.

Stamping on fabric and ceramics

Only natural textiles such as unbleached cotton and linen should be used for printing with stamps. Fabric paint must be fixed by ironing on the reverse side, while ceramic paint has to be fixed by baking it in an oven.

Looking after your stamps and ink pads

To make your stamps last, be sure to wipe them clean every time you change colours. Use kitchen paper or a kneaded rubber, and make sure you clean out all the cracks. Always check that there is no paint residue on the stamp before applying it to a fresh surface. The trick is never to allow the paint or ink to dry, so rinse the stamp as soon as you finish using it. If necessary, you can gently clean it with a toothbrush and washing-up liquid, before pressing out any remaining colour on a dry cloth and leaving the stamp to dry in the open air.

If ink does dry on a stamp, you can try washing it in soapy water or with specialist stamp cleaner, which is sold in craft shops. Rub this directly onto the rubber stamp with a clean cloth.

Ink pads should be stored upside down to keep the ink on the surface of the pad. You can refill ink pads as needed, and you can also make your own pads from specially designed stamp pad foam.

Choosing a colour scheme

Scandinavian-style pastels suit almost any interior. One such colour is celadon green, which can be obtained by mixing spring green with turquoise and white, while coral is a combination of orange, shocking pink and a dash of yellow that can be altered with the addition of grey, white or more yellow.

Darker colours (such as ultramarine, petrol blue, brick red or black) are perfect for setting off a minimalist grey or white interior. Another option is mustard, which you can mix by combining golden yellow and khaki. You can also add a splash of bright orange or pink for a more modern look.

Finally, do not forget that a light-coloured background will help to make your motifs stand out strongly.

LITTLE FISH

Level of difficulty
Medium

Time required to make the stamp
15 mins

Time required to stamp the pillowcase and duvet cover
2 hrs + 1 hr for drying
  + 1 hr for fixing the
  colour

Materials
1 pillowcase
1 duvet cover
1 sheet of craft lino
Large piece of cardboard
Fabric paint in grey,
  green, yellow and red
Paintbrush
Kitchen paper
Black felt-tip pen
V gouge
Craft knife
Iron
Tracing paper
Pencil
Scissors
Ruler

Good to know
You can also use this
technique on paper.

A simple linocut stamp is an easy way of brightening up your bed linen.

How to make the stamp

1. Trace the fish template on page 68. Cut it out and transfer its outline and details onto the sheet of lino.

2. Using the V gouge, first go around the outline of the fish and then mark the scales and other details, pressing firmly. Hold the tip of the craft knife vertically over the fish's eye, and turn it in a circle to make a clean hole.

3. Draw a rectangle around the fish and gouge away the lino between the fish outline and the border of the rectangle. This will ensure that the fish prints clearly.

4. Cut out the rectangle around the fish. This will be your stamp.

Instructions

1. On the reverse side of the stamp, mark a T over the middle of the tail and an M over the mouth. This will make it easier to position each fish in relation to the others.

2. Use the felt-tip to draw a rectangle the same size as the pillowcase on a piece of cardboard. Draw a spiral on the cardboard, working from the centre outwards. Slide the cardboard inside the pillowcase.

LITTLE FISH

(continued)

3. Apply fabric paint to the fish stamp with the brush and print the first fish in the centre of the pillowcase.

4. Wipe off the paint to change colour. Print a second fish about 2 cm away from the first, using the spiral as a guide. Repeat this process, swapping between the four colours.

5. When you reach the penultimate ring of the spiral, leave a space of about 3 cm between each fish.

6. On the final outer ring of the spiral, space the fish roughly 7 cm apart.

7. Take the duvet cover and print a row of fish, 4 cm apart from each other, along the top, first on one side and then on the other. Repeat this process, printing a second row across the middle of the duvet cover and a third across the bottom.

8. Leave to dry for 1 hr and then iron the motifs on the reverse side, using the cotton setting.

POLKA-DOT CURTAIN

Level of difficulty
Easy

Time required
1 hr + 1 hr for drying
  + 5 mins for fixing

Materials
1 cotton curtain
5 corks
Fabric paint in pink,
  gold, grey, blue
  and green
Iron

Polka dots transform a simple curtain into a stylish way to hide a clothes rail, decorate a doorway or add a distinctive touch to a bathroom. Polka dots are elegant and never go out of style - and bold colours will brighten up any setting.

How to make the stamp

1. Make sure you have a separate cork for each colour.

2. Dip the end of the cork into paint and press the cork on the curtain.

3. Alternate the five colours.

Instructions

1. Work across the curtain horizontally rather than vertically - this will allow you to see the overall effect more clearly. Try to vary the spacing between the dots, with some widely scattered and others bunched together.

2. Leave to dry for 1 hr and then iron the motifs on the reverse side, using the cotton setting.

Good to know
Corks can also be used to print polka dots on paper (to make gift wrapping, for example). You can also carve a motif out of the end of the cork.

Sew it yourself
To make a curtain from scratch, you will need 250 × 150 cm of cotton. Cut a piece measuring 150 × 225 cm for the main panel and 11 strips of 4 × 60 cm for the ties. Hem the edges of the panel, then hem the edges of the ties and attach them to one edge of the curtain, leaving 16 cm gaps between each one.

GEOMETRIC CUSHIONS

Level of difficulty
Easy

Time required to make the stamp
30 mins

Time required for the cross-motif cushion
15 mins + 1 hr for drying + 5 mins for fixing

Time required for the half-moon cushion
20 mins + 1 hr for drying + 5 mins for fixing

Materials
2 plain cushion covers
1 large potato
Knife with sharp point
Kitchen paper
Cardboard
Dressmaker's pencil
Fabric paint in pink
   (for the cross-motif
   cushion) or black,
   yellow and green (for
   the half-moon cushion
Iron
Tracing paper
Pencil
Scissors
Ruler

The versatility of the potato never ceases to amaze - and here's the proof!

How to make the stamps

1. Cut the potato in half lengthwise.

2. Trace the half-moon and cross motifs from page 68 and cut them out.

3. Put one cut-out on each face of the potato and carve around its outline with the knife, cutting to a depth of 1 cm.

4. Remove the potato flesh around the outline by making horizontal cuts.

5. Leave the potato halves face down on kitchen paper for 30 mins to draw out any moisture.

Instructions

1. Slide a piece of cardboard inside a cushion cover to provide a stiff base.

2. To create the half-moon design, draw several lines from one end of the cushion to the other with a dressmaker's pencil and ruler, spacing the lines 4 cm apart.

3. Apply a generous coat of black paint to the half-moon stamp and press it firmly onto the cushion, working from the left along the first pencilled line. Reapply paint and repeat the process until the whole line is complete.

4. Remove the potato and clean as necessary.

GEOMETRIC CUSHIONS

(continued)

5. Repeat the process along all but the third and fifth rows. Use the yellow paint on the third row and the green paint on the fifth row, or combine all three colours in any combination you want.

6. Brush off any remaining pencil lines.

7. Leave to dry for 1 hr and then iron the motifs on the reverse side for 5 mins, using the cotton setting.

8. To make the cross design, follow the same steps but space the rows 3 cm apart.

BAGS FOR BITS AND BOBS

Level of difficulty
Medium

Time required to make
one stamp
15 mins

Time required to stamp
one bag
5 mins + 1 hr for drying
+ 15 secs for fixing

Materials
Plain drawstring bags
  in unbleached cotton
Lino for printing
Ink pads for textiles
  in green, grey, blue
  and pink
1 V gouge
1 square gouge
Craft knife
Polymer clay
Alphabet pasta shapes
1 ballpoint pen
1 lino roller
Iron
Greaseproof paper
Pencil
Tracing paper

These bags are a great storage idea.

How to make the stamps

1. Trace the templates from page 68 with the pencil and transfer them onto the lino. Go over the outlines with the ballpoint pen.

2. Use the V gouge to go around the pen outlines and then go over them again, this time exerting more pressure.

3. Use the square gouge to hollow out the empty spaces inside the motifs. To make the buttonholes, position the craft knife point downwards and gently turn it. Gouge away the lino around the motifs to create the stamp.

Instructions

1. Press the ink pad against a stamp.

2. Place the stamp on the bag, and press down the stamp with the roller.

3. To name each bag, use the alphabet shapes to spell a word such as 'glasses' or 'buttons'. Flip the letters over so the word appears in reverse.

4. Make a strip of polymer clay around 1 cm thick, and press the reversed letters into it, standing clear of the clay. Bake the clay according to the package instructions to harden it.

5. Ink the lettered stamp and press it firmly onto the bag.

6. Leave the bag to dry for 1 hr and then iron the motifs, covering them with greaseproof paper first.

POLKA-DOT TABLEWARE

Level of difficulty
Easy

Time required for the plate
10 mins + 24 hrs for
  drying + 35 mins for
  baking

Time required for the mug
15 mins + 24 hrs for
  drying + 35 mins for
  baking

Materials
1 ceramic plate
2 ceramic mugs
2 foam paint pouncers with
  circular ends (1 large
  and 1 small)
Pencil with a rubber on
  the end
Black and gold ceramic
  paint (water soluble)
Paint mixing sticks
Clean tea towel

A pencil rubber and a little paint are all you need to spruce up your plain white ceramics with stylish black or gold dots.

To make the plate

1. Wash the plate in soapy water and dry it with a tea towel.

2. Mix the paint with a stick, stirring gently to prevent air bubbles.

3. Pour the paint into a container and soak the tip of the large pouncer in it. Remove any excess paint.

4. Press the pouncer onto the plate, rocking it forwards and backwards. Don't press too hard, otherwise air bubbles may form. Print two more large dots in the same way. Then use the small pouncer to make three smaller dots.

5. Leave to dry for 24 hrs.

6. Place the plate in an unheated oven and turn it on; once the temperature reaches 150°C (gas mark 2), leave the plate to bake for a further 35 mins. The plate is now dishwasher-safe.

To make the mug with black dots

1. Follow steps 1-3 for the plate (above), soaking the tip of the small pouncer in the paint.

2. Place the mug on its side and press it with the small pouncer, rocking it forwards and backwards. Don't press too hard, otherwise air bubbles may form. Wait for one dot to dry (at least

20 secs) before adding the next one. Turn the mug gently to prevent the paint from running.

3. Follow the same process for every dot until the mug is fully decorated.

4. Leave to dry for 24 hrs.

5. Place the mug in an unheated oven and turn it on; once the temperature reaches 150°C (gas mark 2), leave the mug to bake for a further 35 mins. The mug is now dishwasher-safe.

To make the mug with gold dots

1. Follow steps 1-2 for the plate (page 23).

2. Place the mug on its side. Soak the rubber tip of the pencil in the gold paint and press it on the mug. Wait until the paint dries (at least 20 secs) before adding the next dot. Turn the mug gently to prevent the paint from running.

3. Follow the same process for every dot until the mug is fully decorated.

4. Leave to dry for 24 hrs.

5. Place the mug in an unheated oven and turn it on; once the temperature reaches 150°C (gas mark 2), leave the mug to bake for a further 35 mins. The mug is now dishwasher-safe.

TOO HOT TO HANDLE

Level of difficulty
Easy

Time required to make the stamp
5 mins

Time required to print a coaster
15 mins + 24 hrs for
 drying

Materials
2 coasters made of cork
White rectangular
 pencil rubber
Craft knife
Ruler
Acrylic paint in yellow,
 white and red
Paintbrush
Paper plates

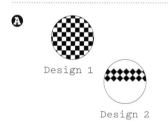

Ⓐ

Design 1

Design 2

Tip
Clean the rubber thoroughly
before changing colours.

A pencil rubber and some acrylic paint can bring a touch of colour to any kitchen.

To make the stamp

Using a craft knife and a ruler, cut the pencil rubber into a neat square.

To make the yellow chequerboard coaster

1. Pour some yellow paint onto a paper plate. Dip the square stamp into it and press it firmly against the coaster. Repeat the process to create a chequerboard effect over the entire coaster, as shown in diagram **Ⓐ**.

2. If needed, stamp over the squares a second time to keep the colour bold.

To make the red coaster

1. Paint the coaster red and leave to dry.

2. Pour some white paint onto a paper plate. Dip the square stamp into it and rotate the square 45 degrees to make a diamond shape. Press it against the coaster firmly to create a row of white diamonds. Clean the stamp thoroughly. Now put some yellow paint on a paper plate and stamp a second row of diamonds, making sure the staggered rows align neatly. Repeat the process to make four rows of diamonds in alternating colours.

TRIANGLE TRAY

Level of difficulty
Medium

Time required to make the stamps
5 mins

Time required to stamp the tray
20 mins

Materials
1 wooden tray, 25 × 18 cm
1 foam sheet
Gouache paint in grey,
   orange and green
Double-sided sticky tape
3 flat paintbrushes
3 clear acrylic stamping
   blocks (or an acrylic
   sheet that can be cut
   into blocks)
Water-based matt varnish
Scissors
Pencil
Ruler

Use foam stamps to personalize a wooden tray with a pretty geometric design.

To make the stamp

1. Mark out three triangles on the foam sheet using the pencil and ruler. Each triangle should have a base measuring 3.5 cm and two sides measuring 3 cm.

2. Cover one side of each triangle with double-sided tape and cut off any excess.

3. Use the tape to stick the triangles onto the acrylic stamping blocks.

Instructions

1. Plan the design for your tray, using the pattern shown in diagram **Ⓐ** as a guide and taking the size of your tray into account. In the top left corner of your tray, place two triangles together along their bases to make a diamond shape, keeping as close to the edge of the tray as possible. Use a pencil to mark the four corners of the diamond. Using these marks as a guide, move the diamond vertically to start building a vertical row. Repeat the process, building the column down the left-hand edge of the tray first, then moving horizontally across the tray until the whole design has been mapped out.

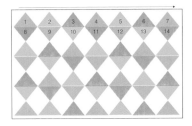

Good to know
The foam stamps used in this design are also good for stamping patterns onto paper.

TRIANGLE TRAY

(continued)

2. Use a brush to apply paint to one of the foam triangles and press the stamp against the tray, starting in the top left corner, with the triangle pointing upwards like a pyramid. If you put just a little paint on the stamp, the motif will look soft and stippled. In contrast, a heavier application of paint will print a much bolder shape. It's a good idea to alternate these two effects to give the design variety. Alternate between the three colours, as shown in diagram **Ⓐ** on page 28. On a 25 × 18 cm tray, the first row will consist of seven triangles.

3. Repeat the process to create the second row of triangles, this time pointing downwards. Keep alternating the three colours.

4. Repeat steps 2 and 3 to make five more rows of triangles, filling the tray completely.

5. Paint the edge of the tray to create a coloured border.

6. Apply a coat of protective varnish to the surface of the tray.

APPLE APRON

Level of difficulty
Easy

**Time required to make
the stamp**
30 mins

**Time required to stamp
the apron**
20 mins + 1 hr for drying
+ 15 secs for fixing
the colour

Materials
1 plain kitchen apron
1 apple (medium-sized,
regular shape, with
an attractive stem)
Fabric paint in blue
and green
Kitchen paper
Fine paintbrush
Medium-sized paintbrush
Tailor's chalk
Knife with sharp point
Tracing paper
Greaseproof paper
Pencil
Scissors
Iron

Good to know
This technique can also be
used to decorate stationery
or create pictures.

Transform a plain apron by printing
with an apple. The same design would
also look good on tea towels.

To make the stamp

1. Remove the stem from the apple
and reserve. Cut the apple in two
and remove the pips.

2. Trace the leaf motif from page 68
and cut it out. Place the template
against one half of the apple, near
the edge, and cut away the negative
space around the leaf.

3. Put the apple halves face down on
kitchen paper to draw out any moisture.
Leave for 30 mins.

Instructions

1. Make small marks with chalk along
the bottom of the apron to show where
you want to put the motifs. Space the
marks evenly to get a neat result.

2. Apply a generous coat of the blue
paint to the intact half of the apple.

3. Press the entire face of the apple
onto the apron, evenly and firmly. If
the motif looks patchy, dab on extra
paint with the medium-sized paintbrush
until it's even.

4. Apply green paint to the stem.
Place it carefully on the fabric
and apply gentle pressure.

5. Wipe the outer edge of the apple
clean.

APPLE APRON

(continued)

6. Touch up the hole in the centre of the apple print with the fine paintbrush. If you like, you can also paint a line down the centre to form a heart shape. Repeat the process to make a row of motifs along the bottom of the apron, with a single motif at the top in the centre of the apron's bib.

7. Apply light green paint to the leaf carved into the other half of the apple and print it close to the stem.

8. Leave to dry for 1 hr and then iron the motifs to set them (15 secs for each one), covering them with greaseproof paper first.

DINNER IS SERVED

Level of difficulty
Medium
Time required to make the stamps
10 mins
Time required to stamp the napkin
10 mins + 1 hr for drying
  + 1 min for fixing
  the colour
Materials
Fabric table napkins
1 foam sheet
Pencil
1 black ink pad for
  textiles
1 white ink pad for
  textiles
Piece of wood around
  16 cm long and 7-8 cm
  wide (e.g. a piece of
  skirting board)
Tailor's chalk
Contact glue
Iron
Greaseproof paper
Scissors
Tracing paper
Needle and red stranded
  embroidery thread
  (optional)
Ruler

Good to know
This foam stamp could also be used on paper, metal or wood, perhaps on a wooden tray as shown on page 28.

Plain napkins can be transformed with a few pieces of foam stuck onto wooden blocks. The cutlery motifs are enhanced by the use of two different colours.

To make the stamp

1. Trace the knife and fork motifs from page 69 and cut them out.

2. Place the paper templates on the foam, draw around them with a pencil and cut them out.

3. Apply contact glue to the foam motifs. Leave them for a few minutes and then stick them side by side on the piece of wood (the knife on the left and the fork on the right).

Instructions

1. Use the chalk to draw a straight line parallel with the hem of the napkin to mark the position for your motif.

2. Press the ink pad onto the foam stamps for about 10 secs. Note: do NOT press the stamps onto the pad!

3. Firmly press the entire surface of the stamp onto the napkin for a few seconds.

4. To decorate the whole edge of the napkin, use the chalk to mark out regular intervals and repeat steps 2 and 3, spacing the motifs roughly 5 cm apart.

DINNER IS SERVED

(continued)

5. Print half the napkins with the black pad and the other half with the white pad, cleaning the stamp carefully before changing colours.

6. Leave the printed napkins to dry for 1 hr and then iron the motifs to fix them (15 secs for each one), covering them with greaseproof paper first.

7. You could also embroider a star in one corner of the napkin, as shown on page 37, using a double strand of cotton embroidery thread.

TIE-DYE TABLECLOTH

Level of difficulty
Easy

Time required
1 hr

Materials
1 coloured linen or
   cotton table runner
Cotton buds
Pure bleach
Tailor's chalk
Ruler

Tip
The end result will depend
on the fabric used. The
tie-dye effect is stronger
on linen as the bleach seeps
into the fabric, while on
cotton, the dots will have
sharper edges.

Sew it yourself
To make your own linen
table runner, cut a strip
of fabric measuring 61 ×
150 cm, or 61 × 140 cm if you
prefer a more rustic effect
with an unhemmed edge. Print
the design before hemming
the runner.

Stamping with bleach creates a tie-dye effect. Try making matching napkins too.

Instructions

1. Mark guidelines in chalk at 2 cm intervals widthwise across the runner.

2. Soak a cotton bud in bleach and press it twice in succession onto the first guideline, tilting the head slightly to increase contact with the fabric. Work across the fabric, bleaching one dot on each line until the row is complete.

3. Make a second row of dots parallel to the first row, but position the dots to fall between those in the first row, as shown in the photograph opposite, rather than in rigid columns.

4. Make the third row of dots align with the first row. Make the fourth row of dots align with the second row.

5. Repeat the process to make a band of six dotted lines, roughly 10 cm wide.

6. Print a second band of six dotted lines, leaving a gap of 10 cm between the first and second bands.

7. Measure 10 cm from the second band, along the length of the runner, and print three more rows of dots.

8. Measure 9 cm from the third band and print a single row of dots.

9. In the centre of the runner, print a band of six dotted lines.

10. Work across the second half of the runner in the same way, so that it mirrors the first.

STRING STRIPES

Level of difficulty
Easy

Time required to make the stamp
5 mins

Time required to stamp a placemat
10 mins + 1 hr for drying
  + 5 mins for fixing
  the colour

Materials
Placemats
122 cm of cotton cord,
  1 cm thick
Blue fabric paint
Block of wood or sanding
  block
Paintbrush
Contact glue
Iron
Greaseproof paper
Scissors

Good to know
This printing technique can
also be used on paper, metal
or wood.

Sew it yourself
To make a placemat from
scratch, cut two rectangles
of plain cotton measuring 33
× 42 cm. Print one rectangle
with string, as described
on the right. Arrange the
rectangles with right sides
facing, and pin 145 cm of
ready-made yellow piping
around the edges. Stitch
the edges closed, leaving
a 10-cm opening on one side.
Turn the mat the right way
round through the opening
and stitch up the gap.

Textured blue stripes give these placemats a nautical look.

To make the stamp

Wind the length of cord six times around the block of wood, spacing the loops evenly. Glue the ends to the back of the block. The thickness of the cord will determine the width of the stripes. Unlike plain string, cotton cord absorbs paint, and so will produce clearer lines.

Instructions

1. Use a brush to apply paint to the cord. Do not worry about applying the paint evenly: variations in the thickness of the coating will create a more textured effect.

2. Press the stamp onto the placemat, starting in the top left corner and applying even pressure so that the whole length of the cord comes into contact with the fabric, to create a row of vertical lines.

3. Repeat this process, working across the top and bottom of the placemat.

4. Cut one loop of cord off the stamp.

5. Turn the stamp so that the cord now runs horizontally. Press the stamp onto each side of the placemat, twice on the left and twice on the right.

6. Leave to dry for 1 hr and then iron the motifs for 5 mins, covering them with greaseproof paper first.

RUSTIC LANDSCAPES

Level of difficulty
Easy

Time required to make the stamps
15 mins

Time required to make the large picture
25 mins + 10 mins for
  drying

Time required to make the small picture
15 mins + 10 mins for
  drying

Materials
1 sheet of A3 textured
  white drawing paper,
  224 gsm
Ruler
Coloured felt-tip pen
1 sheet of foam, 20 ×
  29 cm
Craft knife
Scissors
Double-sided sticky tape
Acrylic stamping blocks
  (or use old building
  blocks or lids)
Ink pads in black and
  pink
Paintbrush
1 small frame, 18 × 24 cm
1 large frame, 30 × 40 cm

Stamps cut from foam create a simple but charming winter scene, livened up with a touch of pink.

To make the stamps

1. Use the felt-tip pen to copy the motifs from page 70 onto the foam sheet. There are seven different houses, two clouds and a tree.

2. Cut out the shapes with scissors and cut out the windows of the houses with the craft knife.

3. Fix the stamps onto the stamping blocks with double-sided tape.

To make the small picture

1. Take the sheet of drawing paper and cut off a piece measuring 9.5 × 15 cm.

2. Use the two cloud stamps, the tree, and three of the house stamps (nos. 4, 8 and 10). Press the black ink pad onto each stamp several times. Note: do NOT press the stamp onto the pad! Press the stamps onto the paper, using diagram **Ⓐ** on page 47 as a guide.

3. Use the tip of the paintbrush handle to print the puffs of smoke coming out of the chimney by pressing the handle into the pink ink pad and onto the surface of the paper.

4. Leave to dry for at least 20 mins before framing.

RUSTIC LANDSCAPES

(continued)

To make the large picture

1. Cut the A3 sheet of drawing paper in half to make an A4 sheet.

2. Take a stamp and press the black ink pad onto the foam several times. Note: do NOT press the stamps onto the pad! Press the stamp onto the paper. Use diagram **B** as a guide, starting in the bottom left corner and working upwards.

3. Leave to dry for at least 20 mins before framing.

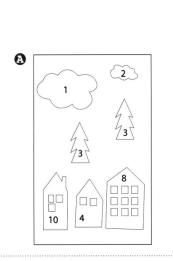

LACE ON METAL

Level of difficulty
Medium

**Time required to make
one printed tin**
15 mins + 2 hrs for
   drying

Materials
Sandpaper
Metal tins with lids
Green and white spray
   paint
Repositionable spray glue
Piece of lace or old net
   curtain
Scissors

**Breathe new life into plain metal tins
by embellishing them with striking
lace motifs.**

Instructions

1. Lightly sand down the metal tins
and their lids.

2. Spray one tin white and the other
tin green. Leave to dry for a minimum
of 2 hrs.

3. Cut the lace or curtain fabric to
fit the tins. Choose bold geometric
or floral designs for the best results.

4. Stick the lace or curtain on the
tins using repositionable spray glue.

5. Gently apply the spray paint, using
green paint for the white tin, and
white paint for the green tin.

6. Remove the lace immediately and
then leave the tins to dry for a
minimum of 1 hr.

Good to know
Motifs can be printed in this
way on all types of support:
paper, metal, textiles, wood
or terracotta.

FALLEN LEAVES

Level of difficulty
Medium

Time required to stamp a plant pot
5-8 mins (depending on
   the motif) + 2 hrs for
   pressing leaves

Materials
Ceramic plant pot
Fresh leaves from a tree
Black and white acrylic
   paint
Flat paintbrush
Kitchen paper
Water-based matt varnish

Good to know
Leaves can also be used to
print on paper, or if fabric
paint is used, onto curtains
or cushions.

Spruce up your plant pots by taking advantage of what nature has to offer. Leaves offer a huge variety of distinctive motifs.

Instructions

1. For the best effect, choose leaves that are flexible, with heavy veins.

2. Place the leaves under a pile of books for at least 2 hrs to press them.

3. Mix the white and black paints to make several different shades of grey (dark for a pale pot, pale for a dark one). If you want a more rustic effect, you can repaint the pots by rubbing them roughly with a cloth soaked in acrylic paint and allowing it to dry before applying the leaf motifs.

4. Apply paint to the veined side of the leaves with the flat brush. Make sure the layer of paint is thin enough to allow the veins to stand out.

5. Press a leaf against the pot, smoothing it with your fingers to ensure that it sticks evenly. Gently peel it off.

6. Repeat this process to cover the whole pot. To make the veins stand out more, dab the leaf with kitchen paper to absorb the excess paint before pressing it against the pot.

7. Allow the pot to dry and then varnish it.

RETRO CHIC

Level of difficulty
Medium

Time required
20 mins

Materials
1 plain lampshade
Cardboard tube from a
   roll of kitchen paper
   (you can use a toilet
   roll tube but you will
   need several, as paint
   softens the cardboard)
Red fabric paint
Kitchen paper
Paintbrush
Scissors
Sticky tape

A cardboard tube from a roll of kitchen paper is an easy way to print a pattern of loose circles.

Instructions

1. Apply paint to the edge of the cardboard tube. Use it to print a circle, starting at the top of the lampshade. As it is not a flat surface, you will have to tilt the tube slightly. Repeat the process until you've made a row of circles around the top of the lampshade. Wipe the inside of the tube from time to time to remove any excess paint.

2. Print the second row of circles, creating a staggered pattern.

3. Repeat this process until the lampshade is covered with several rows of circles.

4. If the circles don't fit neatly along the seam at the back of the lampshade, you can adjust the circumference of the tube by slitting it lengthwise and taping it closed at the size required.

Good to know
Cardboard tubes can also be used to print on paper or wood.

Tip
You can make a heart-shape motif by pinching one side of the tube and stapling it.

RAINDROP DOORMAT

Level of difficulty
Medium

**Time required to make
the stencil**
20 mins

**Time required to stamp
the doormat**
15 mins + 2 hrs for
   drying

Materials
1 doormat
Sheets of paper
Spray paint in black
   and green
Repositionable spray glue
Craft knife
Sticky tape
Ruler
Pencil
Tracing paper
Scissors

Good to know
A stencil can be applied to
any surface if you stick it
in place with spray glue.

**This stencil technique is great for
decorating rough and uneven surfaces.**

To make the stencil

1. Cut a piece of paper the same size
as the doormat.

2. Draw six horizontal lines across
the width of the paper, 6 cm apart.

3. Trace the raindrop motif from
page 71 and cut it out. Using the lines
on the large sheet as a guide, draw
around it as many times as you like,
creating a pattern of drops.

4. Use the craft knife to cut out the
raindrop-shaped holes.

Instructions

1. Spray a generous layer of glue onto
the paper and stick it on the doormat.

2. Work out which raindrops you
want to be green and use the tape
to stick paper rectangles over the
corresponding holes, in order to
mask them.

3. Spray the exposed holes with black
paint and leave to dry for 1 hr.

4. Remove the paper rectangles covering
the unsprayed holes and use paper to
cover the holes that have already been
sprayed with black paint.

5. Spray green paint over the remaining
holes. Remove the stencil and leave to
dry for 1 hr.

STAR-STUDDED SEAT

This upcycled chair would be perfect for a child's bedroom or a hallway.

Level of difficulty
Medium

Time required to make the stamp
5 mins + 12 hrs for
    drying

Time required to stamp the seat
30 mins + 1 hr for drying
    + 5 mins for fixing
    the colour

Materials
1 chair
1 small block of clay
Star-shaped pastry
    cutter
Blue fabric paint
Paintbrush
Cotton fabric
Staple gun or
    hammer + tacks
Kitchen paper
Rolling pin
Iron
Cardboard
Craft knife
Blue acrylic paint
Tape measure

How to make the stamp

1. Knead the clay and roll it to a thickness of 1 cm.

2. Cut out the star motif with the pastry cutter.

3. Leave the star motif to dry under a large book for 24 hrs to flatten it.

Instructions

1. Measure the cotton to fit the size of the seat, allowing a border of 7 cm all the way round (5 cm for the flap underneath and 2 cm for the hem). Cut off the points of all four corners.

2. Apply a generous amount of fabric paint to the star and stamp it on the fabric. After each stamp, carefully wipe its edges and reapply the paint.

3. Leave to dry for 1 hr and then iron the motifs on the reverse side to fix them, using the cotton setting.

4. With the iron, press a 2-cm hem around all the edges of the fabric.

5. Spread the fabric over the chair seat. Fix it in position either by stapling it underneath or hammering in a tack every 2 cm.

6. Draw around the star cutter on cardboard and cut it out with a craft knife to make a stencil. Use it to paint a star on the back of the chair with acrylic paint.

HANGING IN THE AIR

Level of difficulty
Medium

Time required
6-8 mins + 5 mins for
  baking

Materials
56 g of soft white
  polymer clay
Sheet of greaseproof
  paper
Latex gloves (optional)
1 earthenware tile or
  oven tray
Rolling pin
Toothpick
Phillips screwdriver
Piping nozzles (with star
  and circle motifs)
Pastry cutters (circle
  and flower)
1 glass with a decorative
  base
Alphabet pasta shapes

Polymer clay is great for making pretty hanging decorations, stamped with patterns or words. Hang them up with coloured string and patterned sticky tape to add a bright finishing touch.

To make a basic medallion

1. Clean your work surface well and spread greaseproof paper over it.

2. Cut the block of clay into two and knead until the clay is soft. Make two balls and flatten them to a thickness of 2 to 3 mm with a rolling pin. You can prevent marking the clay with fingerprints by wearing latex gloves while you work.

3. Press a pattern into the clay using the screwdriver, piping nozzles or anything else you can find. Cut a shape out of the patterned clay with a pastry cutter. Make a hole for the string with a toothpick, as shown in diagram **Ⓐ**.

4. Heat the oven to 130°C (gas mark 1). Put the greaseproof paper and medallions on a tile or oven tray and bake for 6 mins. Turn the oven off and leave them for a further 3 mins, but remove them earlier if the clay starts to change colour.

To make a message medallion (opposite)

1. Make a sausage with the clay and place it on a sheet of greaseproof paper. Use the rolling pin to flatten it into a strip, 5 mm thick.

Ⓐ

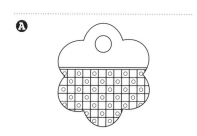

HANGING IN THE AIR

(continued)

2. Spell out a word using the pasta letters and then flip them over, so that the word appears in reverse. Press the letters gently into the polymer clay, so that they stick out. Bake at 130°C (gas mark 1) for 10 mins.

3. Follow steps 1-2 on page 59. Stamp stars with a piping nozzle by pressing its tip into the clay. Leave a space for the word and press the word stamp firmly into the clay.

4. Use a round pastry cutter to cut out the shape. Make a hole with a toothpick. Bake as described on page 59, step 4.

To make a flower medallion (page 58)

Follow steps 1-2 on page 59. Draw a grid over half the surface of the clay with a toothpick. Use a small nozzle with a rounded end to make an imprint in every other square, as shown in diagram **Ⓐ**. Use a pastry cutter to cut out a flower, leaving the top of the shape empty. Make a hole in this area with a toothpick. Bake as described on page 59, step 4.

To make a medallion with radiating lines (opposite)

Follow steps 1-2 on page 59. Find a glass with a decorative base, and press it firmly into the polymer clay. Cut out a medallion with the flower-shaped pastry cutter. Make a hole at the top with a toothpick and bake as described on page 59, step 4.

WRAP IT UP

Level of difficulty
Easy

**Time required to make
the stamp**
8-10 mins

**Time required to print
the wrapping paper**
20 mins + 30-45 mins for
    drying

Materials
Fuse beads
Peg boards for fuse beads
    (square, circular and
    heart-shaped)
Iron
Ironing paper
Acrylic stamping blocks
    (or use old building
    blocks or lids)
Contact glue or glue gun
1 roll of brown paper
Foam block
Acrylic paint in white
    and pink
Scissors

Turn plain brown paper into distinctive
gift wrapping by printing with fuse
beads. It's child's play!

To make a stamp with fuse beads

1. Choose one of the motifs from
page 71: the heart, the arrow, the
anchor or the flower. Copy it by
arranging fuse beads on a peg board.
Cover the beads with a piece of ironing
paper and iron over them in order to
fuse them, following the manufacturer's
instructions. When cooled, take the
beads off the pegboard and turn them
over. Cover with the ironing paper and
press again.

2. Place the fused motif under a heavy
object to keep it flat. Stick it on a
stamping block with a glue gun.

Instructions

1. Cut the brown paper to the desired
size. Keep it flat while you work on
the shiny side.

2. Use the foam block to spread a thin
coat of white or pink acrylic paint on
the fuse-bead stamp.

3. Press the stamp onto the paper,
count to three and then remove it.
Print more motifs all over the paper,
turning them in different directions.

4. Leave to dry for 45 mins.

Tip
Experiment with making fuse-
bead stamps in other shapes.
Try combining different
colours on the same sheet.

IT'S A DATE

Level of difficulty
Easy

Time required
40 mins

Materials
1 roll of brown paper
Ruler
Date stamp
Ink pad
Scissors

Too busy to buy pretty wrapping paper? You can always mark important events with brown paper and the date stamp in the drawer of your desk, and round it off with coloured masking tape.

Instructions

1. Cut the brown paper to the size you want. Keep it flat while you work on the shiny side.

2. Set the date stamp to show the date you want (a birthday, for example).

3. Press the stamp on the ink pad and then onto the paper, count to three and remove it. Repeat as many times as you want. You can arrange the motifs to form lines and squares, or stamp them at random.

4. Leave to dry for at least 10 mins.

PUT A STAMP ON IT

Time required to make the stamp
10 mins

Time required to make an envelope
5 mins + 5 mins for
  drying

Materials
6 pencils with a rubber
  on the end
Craft knife
Several envelopes
Ink pads in grey
  and green

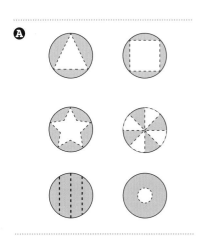

Plain envelopes can be easily embellished with geometric designs. You can vary the effect by using parallel or staggered rows of shapes. Try using fluorescent colours for a change, or white ink on black paper.

**To make the simple stamps
(triangle, star, square, flower)**

Draw a shape on a pencil rubber and use the craft knife to remove the area around the shape, first cutting vertically and then horizontally. Cut each pencil end into a different shape, using diagram **A** as a guide.

To make the more complex stamps

For the circle with vertical lines: draw three lines and cut them out with the craft knife.

For the circle with a hole, place the blade of the craft knife vertically at the centre of the rubber. Turn the pencil (not the blade) in a complete circle, keeping the blade still.

To make the envelopes

1. Decide how you want to arrange the motifs (in parallel lines or in staggered rows). Press your chosen motif against an ink pad and press it against the inside of the envelope.

2. Re-ink the motif after stamping. Repeat until the whole area is covered.

TEMPLATES & MOTIFS

Little fish (page 11)
Actual size

Geometric cushions
(page 16)

Actual size

Geometric cushions
(page 16)

50% size

Bags for bits and bobs (page 20)
50% size

Bags for bits and bobs (page 20)
70% size

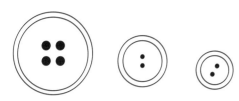

Bags for bits and bobs (page 20)
Actual size

Apple apron (page 32)
Actual size

Dinner is served (page 36)

Actual size

Rustic landscapes (page 44)

Actual size

Raindrop doormat
(page 55)

Actual size

Wrap it up
(page 63)

75% size

ACKNOWLEDGMENTS

We would like to thank all the companies that supplied us with materials for the projects in this book:

Paints for fabrics and ceramics: www.pebeo.com
Lino sheets, clay, ink pads: www.creavea.com
Fabrics: www.mapetitemercerie.com
Fabric ink pads: www.cherie-m.com
Drawstring bags: www.ki-sign.com
Paints: www.eleonore-deco.com
Fluorescent ink pads: www.perlesandco.com

Other suppliers

Candlestick, candles, pear and bird ornaments
(pages 14, 26, 53): Fleux®
Boots (page 54): Aigle®
Jug (page 54): Merci®

A big thank you to:
Karine, my co-pilot: without you, I would never have finished this project. Bring on the next one!
Claire, for those delightful days working together: what an eye!
Lisa, who never had a moment's doubt: for great moments shared, and hopefully more to come.
And Céline, for trusting me.

Émilie

Translated from the French *Les petits ateliers Hachette: Déco au tampon*
by Matthew Clarke

First published in the United Kingdom in 2016 by
Thames & Hudson Ltd, 181A High Holborn, London WC1V 7QX

Original edition © 2015 Hachette Livre (Hachette Pratique), Paris
This edition © 2016 Thames & Hudson Ltd, London

British Library Cataloguing-in-Publication Data
A catalogue record for this book is available from the British Library

ISBN 978-0-500-51845-8

Printed in Spain

To find out about all our publications, please visit **www.thamesandhudson.com**.
There you can subscribe to our e-newsletter, browse or download our current catalogue,
and buy any titles that are in print.